BRILLIANT BLACK BRITISH HISTORY

Written by

Atinuke

Illustrated by

Kingsley Nebechi

BLOOMSBURY
CHILDREN'S BOOKS
LONDON   OXFORD   NEW YORK   NEW DELHI   SYDNEY

"If you know your history, then you would know where you're coming from. Then you wouldn't have to ask me, 'Who the heck do I think I am?'"
Bob Marley

To the children of Britain. Seek out your history – A

For my father. Thank you for your guidance when I needed it the most – K.N.

BLOOMSBURY CHILDREN'S BOOKS
Bloomsbury Publishing Plc
50 Bedford Square, London WC1B 3DP, UK
29 Earlsfort Terrace, Dublin 2, Ireland

BLOOMSBURY, BLOOMSBURY CHILDREN'S BOOKS
and the Diana logo are trademarks
of Bloomsbury Publishing Plc
First published in Great Britain 2023 by
Bloomsbury Publishing Plc
This paperback edition first published in 2024
Text copyright © Atinuke, 2023
Illustrations copyright © Kingsley Nebechi, 2023
World flags and map outlines © Shutterstock
Atinuke and Kingsley Nebechi have asserted
their rights under the Copyright, Designs and
Patents Act, 1988, to be identified as Author and
Illustrator of this work

ISBN: HB: 978-1-5266-3571-6
PB: 978-1-5266-5740-4
eBook: 978-1-5266-5266-9
Audio: 978-1-5266-5267-6
2 4 6 8 10 9 7 5 3 1

Printed and bound in China
by Toppan Leefung Printing

To find out more about our authors and books
visit www.bloomsbury.com and
sign up for our newsletters

CONTENTS

INTRODUCTION

This is a book about British history – the history of some grey-green, rainy islands in the North Sea. This is especially a book about a part of that history that is often left out – the history of the Black people of Britain.

Human beings did not evolve in Britain – they migrated, or moved, here in big groups from other countries. Every single British person comes from a migrant who moved here anytime from yesterday to thousands of years ago.

Modern Black British people are those of us whose parents, grandparents or many times great-grandparents migrated to Britain from Africa, sometimes via the Caribbean, America or other countries, over the last few hundred years.

But there were people with black skin in Britain long before that ...

Most of us do not know where our ancestors came from. But the secret is inside us. Our bodies are made up of cells and each cell contains the data for our ancestors. That data is called DNA.

Scientists can test where our ancestors were from and what they looked like, and they have made an amazing discovery: the first migrants to Britain had black skin. Yes, that's right – the very first Britons were black!

Britain was a black and brown country for around 7,500 years before white people came – and during that time the most famous British monument was built – Stonehenge.

Britain has only been a mostly white country for about 4,500 years – a lot less time than it was a black and brown country.

It is thanks to these discoveries made by scientists in their labs, by librarians who look after documents, by historians who study those documents and by archaeologists who dig things up from the past that I was able to write this book ...

Brilliant Black British History!

The whole of Ireland was once part of Great Britain, so some of its history is in this book, too.

HOMO SAPIENS

Our story begins in Africa, more than 300,000 years ago. There, modern humans evolved. Every single person on our planet, no matter what they look like, belongs to the human race, our species – Homo sapiens.

At first, all Homo sapiens had black skin. That's because we had lots of a chemical called melanin in our skin to protect it from the hot African sun.

But Homo sapiens did not all stay in Africa ...

By **50,000** years ago, we made it to Australia.

By **45,000** years ago, we had arrived in Europe.

But along came the Ice Ages, and Europe froze over, trapped in glaciers that were miles high! Homo sapiens had to cling to life.

Back then in Europe the weather was warm, and the forests were full of food for humans to hunt and to gather.

Historians think that more than **100,000** years ago humans migrated to the Middle East. From there, their children and their children's children slowly spread throughout the world.

We are incredible explorers.

We crossed seas on rafts ...

... climbed mountain ranges in moccasin shoes ...

... survived the Ice Ages without houses or central heating ...

Historians think that about **70,000** years ago, we arrived in South Asia then East Asia.

... and took on huge, fierce animals with only spears.

Luckily, we are not just explorers, we are inventors as well. We use our big brains to design new tools to help us survive. And when we need to, we can adapt our bodies in incredible ways.

EVOLUTION

The sun was so hot where the human race evolved in Africa that we needed lots of melanin in our skin to protect it from burning. Melanin blocks out the sun's ultraviolet rays. It also makes skin dark. The more melanin a person has in their skin, the darker it is.

But we actually need ultraviolet rays to make something very important – vitamin D. Without it, our bones don't grow properly and we can get seriously ill.

In places where the sun is super-hot, people can absorb enough ultraviolet rays to make vitamin D, even if they have dark skin.

Human beings eventually migrated from Africa. They settled all over the world, including in places where sunlight is weaker. This was not a problem at first. Humans were hunter-gatherers in those days. They lived on food full of vitamin D – eggs, red meat and oily fish. They did not have to depend solely on the sun.

Then around 11,000 years ago, Homo sapiens invented farming and started eating grains, like rice and wheat. These foods do not have enough vitamin D to keep people healthy in places where the sun's rays aren't so strong. So those people eventually, slowly, evolved.

Human beings have always explored and invented, as well as evolved. Our inventions mean we now live mostly indoors so most people don't get enough vitamin D from the sun. However, we have invented another way to get it – vitamin D tablets!

Evolution is when a living thing changes gradually over thousands and even millions of years in order to survive. Homo sapiens have evolved a lot. As we spread across the planet, our bodies changed depending on where we settled.

In places with damp, cold air, people's noses became longer and narrower, to warm the cold air.

In high mountainous areas where there is not much oxygen, people's lungs became bigger.

And in places where the sunlight is weak, people developed pale skin, which could absorb enough ultraviolet rays to make vitamin D.

Humans evolved in different ways across the planet, but human beings are still all one species: 99.9 per cent of our DNA is the same!

Most people in the world have enough melanin in their skin to darken it – they are the global majority. White people are the global minority.

FIRST BRITONS

The Ice Ages came and went for thousands of years. During that time, Homo sapiens invented tools like bone needles to sew proper clothes that kept us warm.

Then, at last, around 12,000 years ago, the glaciers started to melt and the land in Europe became warm again.

There were no shops in those days and all humans were hunter-gatherers. Men, women and children worked together to get food and make every single thing they had. They moved from place to place, hunting herds of animals and gathering plants as they went.

In those days there was a vast area of lowland linking Europe to Britain. We call this area Doggerland. After the Ice Ages, some humans in Europe crossed Doggerland, following herds of deer and cattle. They were the first Britons! People have lived here ever since.

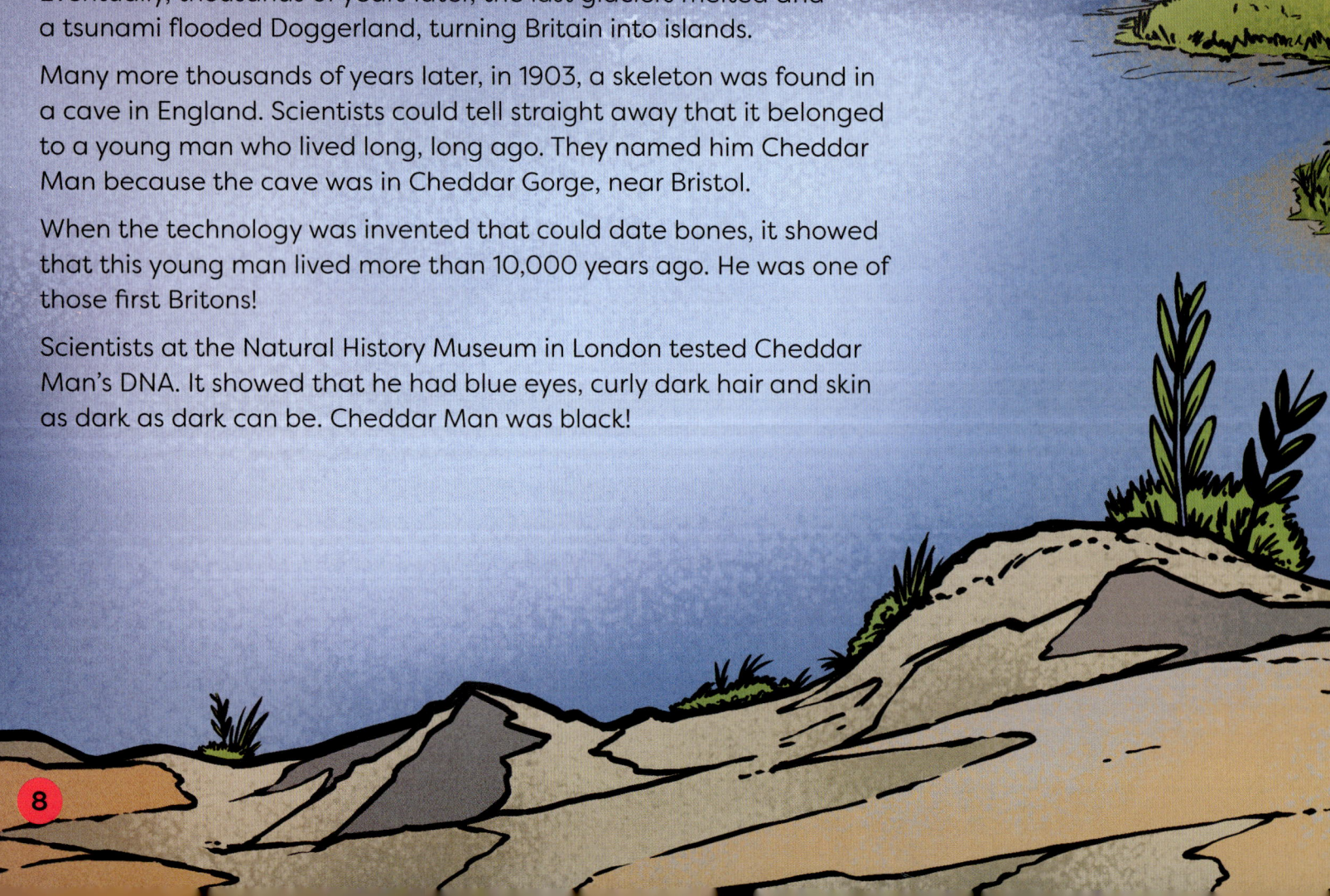

Eventually, thousands of years later, the last glaciers melted and a tsunami flooded Doggerland, turning Britain into islands.

Many more thousands of years later, in 1903, a skeleton was found in a cave in England. Scientists could tell straight away that it belonged to a young man who lived long, long ago. They named him Cheddar Man because the cave was in Cheddar Gorge, near Bristol.

When the technology was invented that could date bones, it showed that this young man lived more than 10,000 years ago. He was one of those first Britons!

Scientists at the Natural History Museum in London tested Cheddar Man's DNA. It showed that he had blue eyes, curly dark hair and skin as dark as dark can be. Cheddar Man was black!

About 12,000 years ago, modern humans settled in Britain. They had black skin – like all Western Europeans in those days. About 6,000 years ago, people with brown skin migrated to Britain. They brought farming and built Stonehenge, in Wiltshire. The first mostly white Britons migrated to Britain about 4,500 years ago. Britain was black for 7,500 years before that!

BRITAIN

There was no civilisation in Britain back then, no towns or cities. But huge stone circles were built that took maths, engineering and the cooperation of big groups of people. Stonehenge is the most famous one. In 2019, scientists did DNA tests on the ethnic group of Britons who built Stonehenge. Some had light brown skin, others dark brown skin.

OLMEC AND MAYAN CIVILISATIONS (Mexico and Central America)

These civilisations were the creators of the best comfort food ever – chocolate!

ANCIENT EGYPT

This African civilisation built pyramids and developed maths, medicine, engineering, astronomy and writing.

FIRST CIVILISATIONS

For nearly 300,000 years, Homo sapiens were hunter-gatherers. We thrived, and so did the planet. But, everything changed around 11,000 years ago when people discovered how to farm!

One farmer could grow enough food for lots of people. And those people were now free to do other things – like invent and develop writing, maths and engineering, and build big buildings.

People stopped moving around all the time and settled in villages around farms. The villages grew into towns, towns into cities, and cities into nations. Nations with rulers to rule them, governments to organise them and armies to protect them.

This is called civilisation!

NOK (modern-day Nigeria)

This African civilisation invented the use of iron to make tools. They also made incredible art.

MESOPOTAMIA (modern-day Iraq)
This Middle Eastern civilisation invented the wonderful wheel!

INDUS VALLEY (modern-day Pakistan, India, Afghanistan)
This Asian civilisation invented flushing toilets, buttons and dice.

ANCIENT CHINA
This Asian civilisation invented gunpowder, fireworks and paper – and built the Great Wall of China.

NUBIA (modern-day Sudan and Egypt)
This African civilisation was ruled by Black pharaohs for almost 100 years.

Civilisations sprang up all around the world from 11,000 years ago onwards. They were all different, but they all depended on farming. They traded with each other, too – not just goods but ideas and inventions as well.

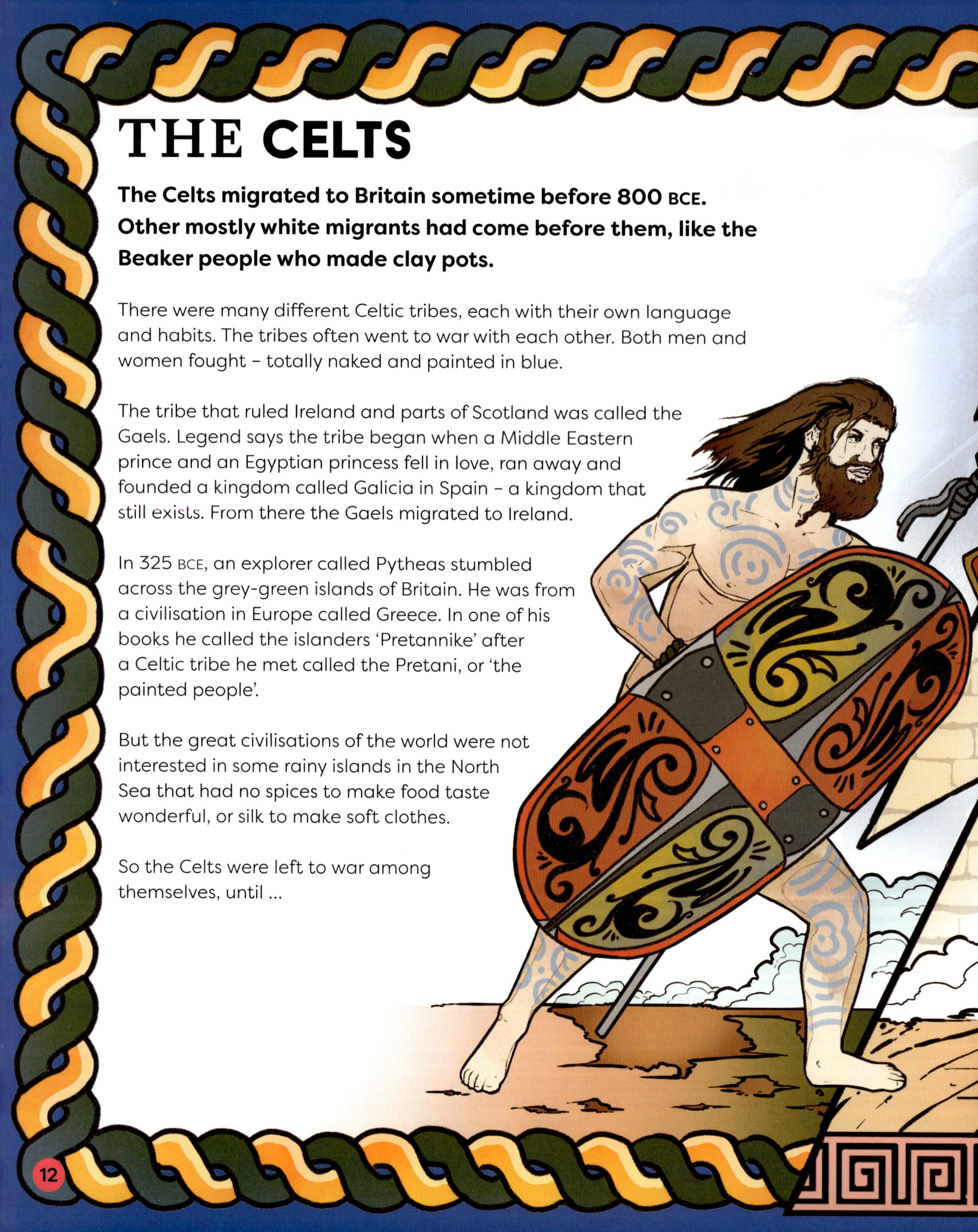

THE CELTS

The Celts migrated to Britain sometime before 800 BCE. Other mostly white migrants had come before them, like the Beaker people who made clay pots.

There were many different Celtic tribes, each with their own language and habits. The tribes often went to war with each other. Both men and women fought – totally naked and painted in blue.

The tribe that ruled Ireland and parts of Scotland was called the Gaels. Legend says the tribe began when a Middle Eastern prince and an Egyptian princess fell in love, ran away and founded a kingdom called Galicia in Spain – a kingdom that still exists. From there the Gaels migrated to Ireland.

In 325 BCE, an explorer called Pytheas stumbled across the grey-green islands of Britain. He was from a civilisation in Europe called Greece. In one of his books he called the islanders 'Pretannike' after a Celtic tribe he met called the Pretani, or 'the painted people'.

But the great civilisations of the world were not interested in some rainy islands in the North Sea that had no spices to make food taste wonderful, or silk to make soft clothes.

So the Celts were left to war among themselves, until …

THE ROMANS

A new civilisation rose in Europe from a small city called Rome. From that city an empire grew and grew and grew. It conquered large parts of Europe, the Middle East and North Africa. The Romans wanted to conquer the whole world ...

... but the Romans could not travel further south than North Africa. In their way was a desert as wide as an ocean and a warrior queen, Amanishakheto of Nubia, who would not let them pass.

The Romans turned back to Europe and pushed north. They headed for some islands lost in rain and mist. Islands they had read about in one of Pytheas's books. Islands they renamed Britannica!

A Roman historian called Tacitus wrote that the Romans found white people from Europe living on the coast of Britannica, while inland lived the original Britons who were dark-skinned and curly-haired.

Roman soldiers were the best in the world, but they shivered in their boots when they faced the warriors who came screaming blue murder out of the lashing British rain.

In the end, the Romans only managed to conquer part of what we now call England and Wales. They never defeated the Cornish, Irish or Scottish tribes.

The part of Britain that the Romans conquered became known as Roman Britain.

The Emperor Hadrian built a wall north of Roman Britain in 122 CE to keep out the ferocious Scottish tribes. The wall was guarded by 500 North African soldiers.

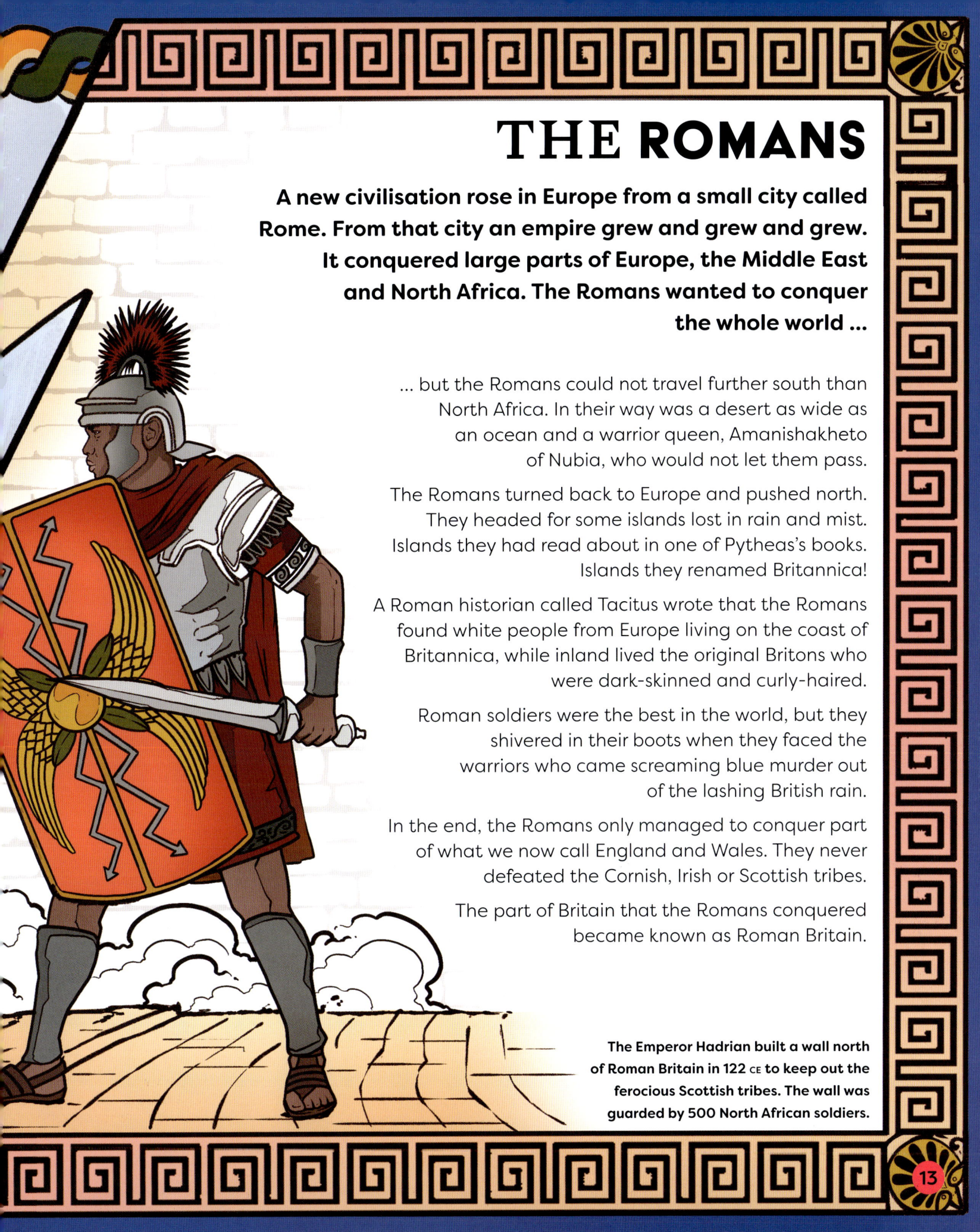

BLACK **ROMAN** BRITAIN

Black, white and brown people lived in the Roman Empire. Anyone who was rich and important could become a Roman citizen – with men having the right to vote and become emperor.

However, it was enslaved people who did all the hard work. Historians think that most enslaved people in the Roman Empire were white and owned by important Black and white Romans.

Britain was ruled by Roman governors who all hoped to become emperor one day. From around 139 to 144 CE, Quintus Lollius Urbicus was the governor of Britain. He was a Berber from North Africa – the first ruler of England and Wales with brown skin.

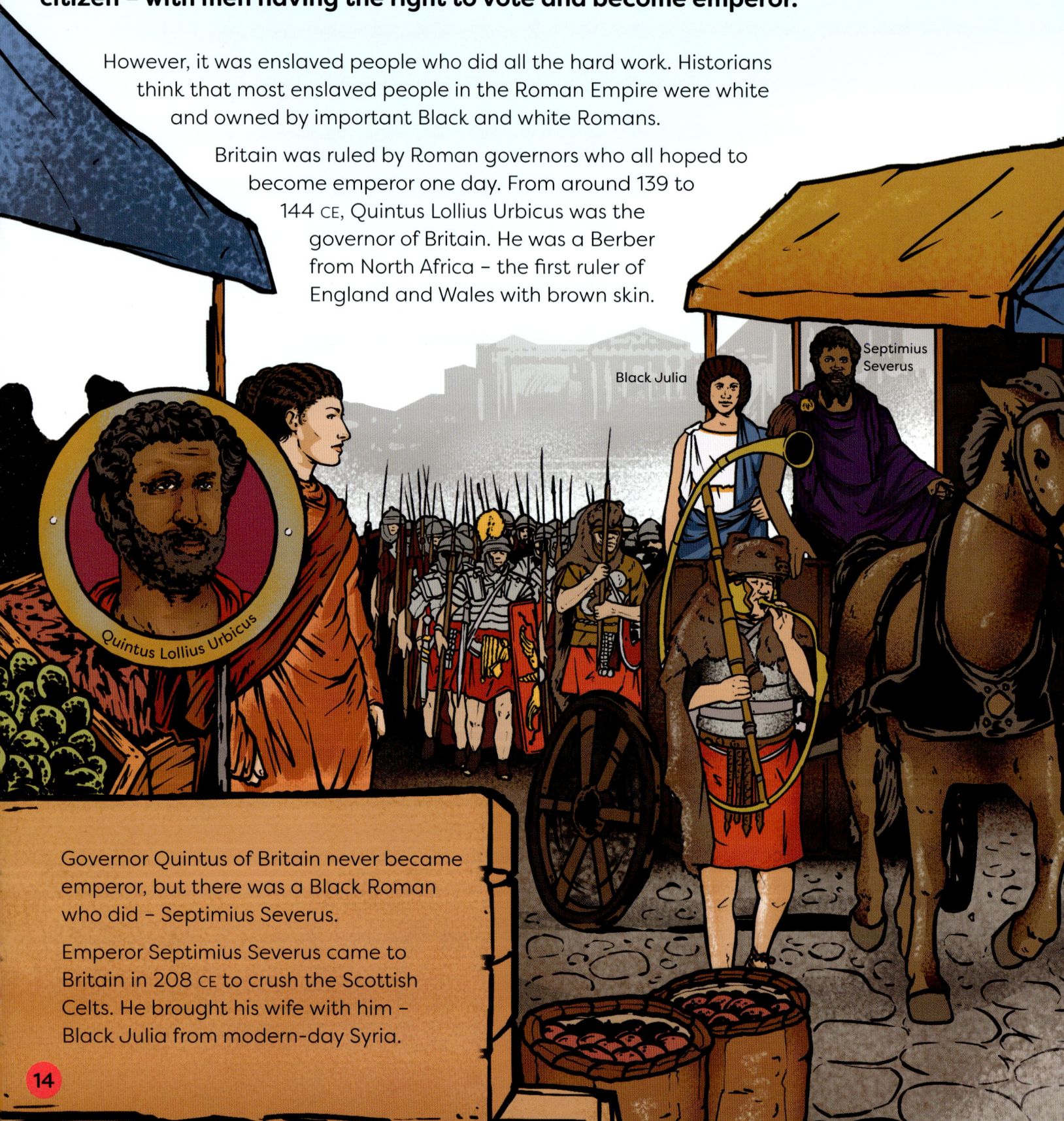

Quintus Lollius Urbicus

Black Julia

Septimius Severus

Governor Quintus of Britain never became emperor, but there was a Black Roman who did – Septimius Severus.

Emperor Septimius Severus came to Britain in 208 CE to crush the Scottish Celts. He brought his wife with him – Black Julia from modern-day Syria.

14

Emperor Septimius Severus and Black Julia ruled the Empire together from York, one of Roman Britain's most important cities.

Septimius never did beat the Scots. After three years of trying, he died in York, England.

HOW DO WE KNOW WHO LIVED IN ROMAN BRITAIN?

We have old documents written by the Romans. DNA tests also tell us that 11 per cent of people in Roman York were Black, with African parents or grandparents. Today, four per cent of people in England and Wales are Black.

In 1901, a rich and important Roman lady was found in a stone coffin in York. In the coffin there was also an African ivory bangle and an English jet bangle. In 2010, DNA tests revealed the lady was of mixed African and British heritage – just like her bangles!

CHRISTIANITY COMES TO BRITAIN

Christianity started when a baby was born in Bethlehem in about the year 1 CE. His name was Jesus.

Bethlehem was in the Jewish Kingdom of Judea, in the Middle East. It was being ruled by Romans. The Jewish people were waiting for a Messiah, or saviour, to get rid of the Romans. When Jesus grew up to be a spiritual teacher, his followers believed that he was the Messiah.

The Romans did not want to be overthrown, so they had Jesus killed. They thought that was the end of it. But it was not ...

Jesus's followers said he had come back to life. They spoke to him, and watched him float up to heaven. They called him Jesus Christ, the son of God. They called themselves Christians.

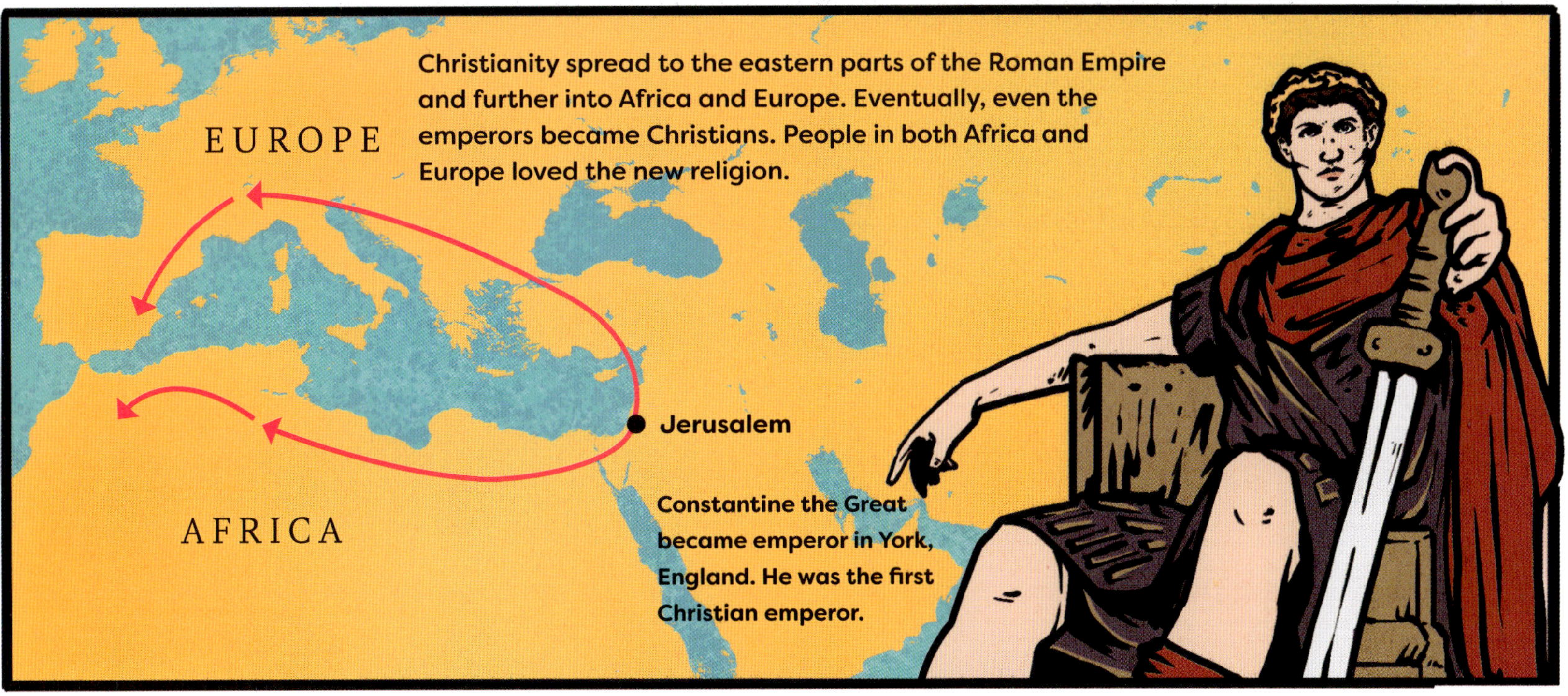

Christianity spread to the eastern parts of the Roman Empire and further into Africa and Europe. Eventually, even the emperors became Christians. People in both Africa and Europe loved the new religion.

EUROPE

Jerusalem

AFRICA

Constantine the Great became emperor in York, England. He was the first Christian emperor.

Some historians say that Ethiopia, in Africa, was the first Christian country in the world. The oldest illustrated Christian book is Ethiopian. Some say their churches are the eighth Wonder of the World.

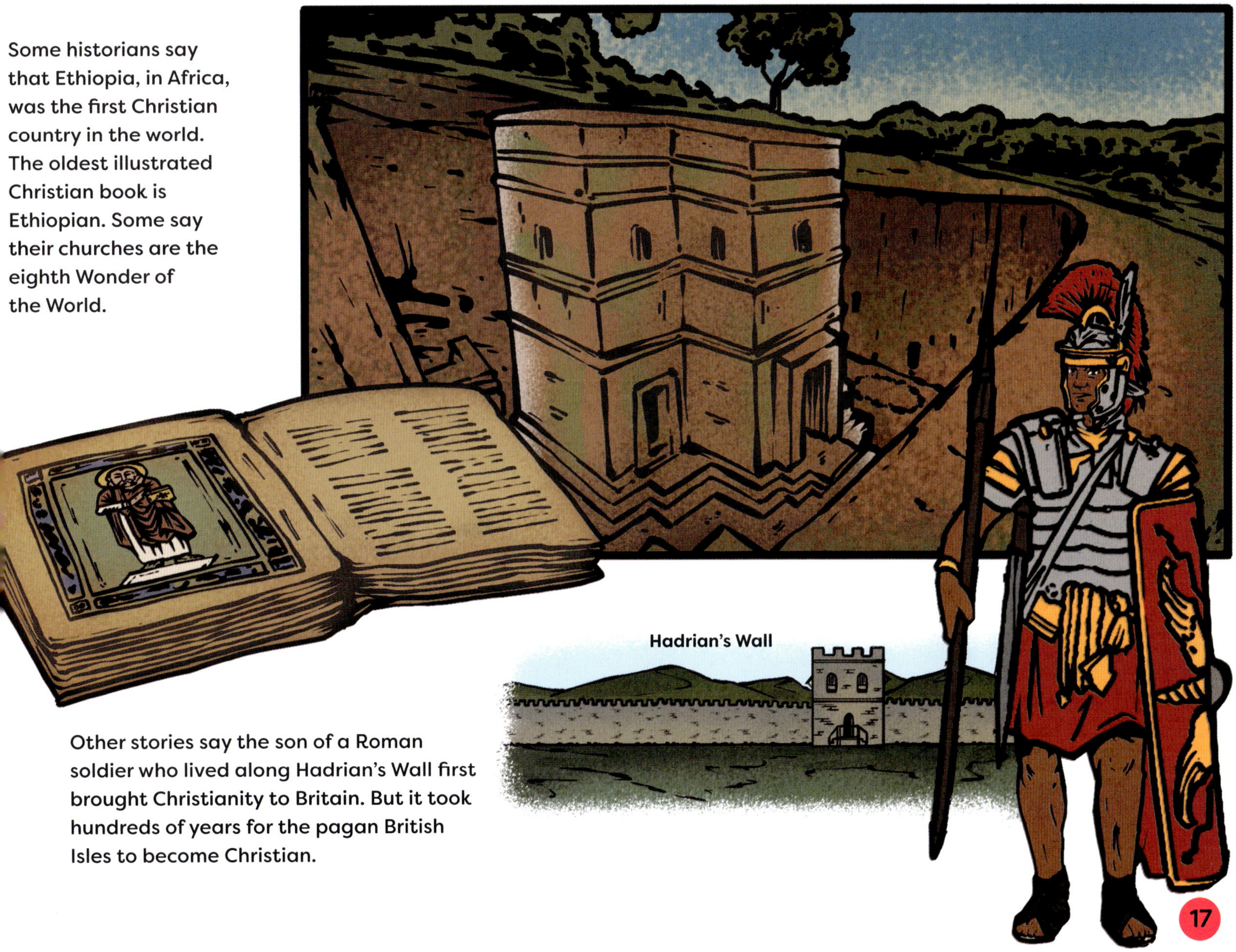

Hadrian's Wall

Other stories say the son of a Roman soldier who lived along Hadrian's Wall first brought Christianity to Britain. But it took hundreds of years for the pagan British Isles to become Christian.

17

CONQUERORS AND MIGRANTS

By the 5th century, the Roman Empire had retreated from Britain and new waves of conquerors and migrants were arriving. So began 1,000 years of war. This was a time when life was short and not sweet, known as the Middle Ages.

The Anglo-Saxon tribes came first. They were white migrants from Northern Europe who came looking for good land to raise their crops and children. These tribes fought each other, and both the Celts and Roman Britons, for hundreds of years.

The Vikings came next – to conquer and get rich quick! And they found something in Britain more valuable than silver and gold to make their fortune: people.

The Vikings enslaved many thousands of Britons – Anglo-Saxons, Celts and Roman Britons – and sold them all over the world. About ten per cent of people in Britain were enslaved – white, Black and brown.

The Vikings also captured a group of Black men in Morocco, Africa, and brought them to live in Ireland in 862 CE. The Irish called them 'blue men'.

DNA tests have been done on some of the skeletons found in Anglo-Saxon graves. One was a rich and noble Anglo-Saxon girl who had a West African grandfather or great-grandfather. Could she have been a West African Anglo-Saxon princess?

One Anglo-Saxon tribe was called the Angles. The kingdom they formed in Britain was called Angle-land – in other words, England!

During the Middle Ages, in 1066, a Norman tribe from France conquered Britain. The Normans built churches and castles all over Britain – and tried to stop people being sold as slaves.

Britons were now a hodgepodge of people: original British migrants, Celts, Roman Britons, Anglo-Saxons, Vikings, Africans and Normans. They spoke a hodgepodge language, too – English!

Bog and **iron** are Celtic and Gaelic words. **Devil**, **angel** and **slave** are Roman Latin words. **Amen**, **pharaoh** and **Satan** are Jewish Hebrew words that came with Christianity. **Cow** and **pig** are Anglo-Saxon words. **Give**, **take** and **die** are Viking words. **Table** and **mansion** are Norman words.

New English words are always just around the corner!

In 2013, two boys playing in a river in Gloucestershire, in the west of England, found a skull. DNA tests showed it belonged to a young Black woman from the Middle Ages.

19

SWEDEN
Vikings have been found buried wearing clothes and jewellery decorated with the words 'La ilaha illa Allah'.

NORTHERN EUROPE
Christian knights rode off to conquer the homeland of Jesus – which was now part of a powerful Islamic Empire. These wars were called The Crusades.

ENGLAND
The mighty Anglo-Saxon King Offa made gold coins that said 'La ilaha illa Allah'.

CAIRO, EGYPT
One of the first modern hospitals in the world was built in Egypt's capital city, Cairo, when it was part of an Islamic empire.

SPAIN, PORTUGAL AND SOUTH-WEST FRANCE
For 800 years, there was a great Islamic Empire here called al-Andalus where discoveries were made in medicine, surgery and architecture.

MECCA, SAUDI ARABIA
Muslims all over the world pray towards the holy city of Mecca. A muezzin is a person who calls Muslims to pray five times a day. The very first muezzin, Bilal ibn Rabah, was Black.

FEZ, MOROCCO
Once, Morocco ruled all of North Africa and Southern Europe. In the city of Fez, the first university in the world was built by Fatima al-Fihri.

MALI, MAURITANIA AND CHAD
The wealthy empires of West Africa converted to Islam and built mosques, libraries and universities in their great cities.

EAST AFRICA
The Somalis were the first people to convert to Islam. Ordinary Muslims in the Swahili city states could read, whereas in Britain most ordinary people could not!

THE RISE OF ISLAM

While Britain was struggling through the Middle Ages, a new religion called Islam had become popular across the world.

Islam began around 610 CE, when it is said an angel appeared to the Prophet Muhammad in a cave near Mecca, now in Saudi Arabia. This angel said there was only one God. Most people in those days believed there were lots of gods – except for some, including Jewish and Christian people. The Muslim creed begins 'La ilaha illa Allah', which means 'there is no god but the one God'.

Islam spread around the world from the Middle East. Soon, many of the great empires of Africa, the Middle East, Europe and Asia were all Islamic.

BAGHDAD, IRAQ
The most advanced city in the world was in Baghdad, where Muslim, Christian, Jewish and Hindu scholars all worked together. They developed trigonometry and algebra. The philosopher al-Jāḥiẓ from East Africa came up with the theory of evolution (1,000 years before Charles Darwin did).

CANTON, CHINA
Traders and important officials brought Islam to China. One of the oldest mosques in the world is here – the Lighthouse Mosque.

INDIA, PAKISTAN AND BANGLADESH
Muslim traders on ships brought Islam to South-East Asia. They learnt the written Hindu numbers 0 to 9 and now everybody uses them!

The English words **giraffe**, **coffee**, **sofa** and **sugar** all come from Arabic.

From the 8th to the 13th century, the Islamic empires were global superpowers. It was the Golden Age of Islam.

Islam has influenced Britain for over 1,000 years. Today, it is Britain's second biggest religion.

TUDORS AND STUARTS

When the Middle Ages were over, Tudor kings and queens ruled England. The English kings before them had conquered the Princes of Wales, double-crossed the High King of Ireland and now they had their eyes on Scotland, ruled by the Stuarts.

There were hundreds of Black Britons in Tudor and Stuart Britain. Many of them were Muslims who migrated to Britain from the Islamic Empires in Europe and Africa. Along with them came new knowledge about textiles, medicine, maths and navigation.

John Blanke, trumpeter in the Tudor court, wrote to Henry VIII demanding a pay rise!

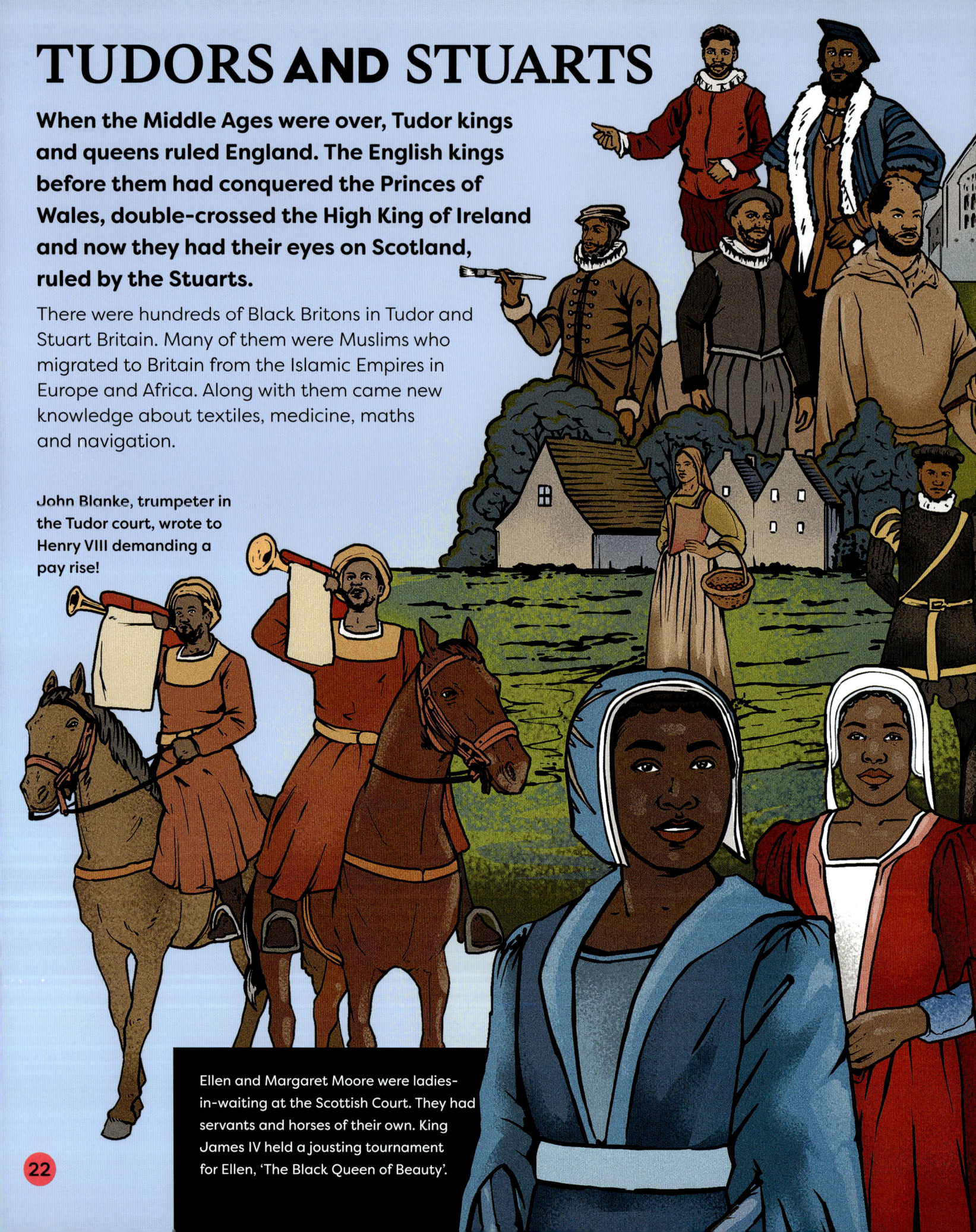

Ellen and Margaret Moore were ladies-in-waiting at the Scottish Court. They had servants and horses of their own. King James IV held a jousting tournament for Ellen, 'The Black Queen of Beauty'.

There were Black milkmaids, monks and musicians, sailors, soldiers and spies, ambassadors and artists, grooms and gardeners, cooks and butlers, ladies and pirates, and more!

Incense was used to cover the stink of potties that were emptied on to the streets!

Popular new goods came into Britain, too: silk from China, spices from Africa and incense from India.

Stories of the fabulous wealth of those continents reached the ears of the new Tudor queen – Elizabeth I. She sent ships to look for India's riches and Africa's gold.

And so began the British Empire.

23

AFRICAN EMPIRES

When British ships landed south of the Sahara in the 1500s, rich and powerful empires and kingdoms covered every inch of Africa.

The British found many cities – some bigger than London was back then. These cities had mosques as big as castles, churches as big as cathedrals, universities full of scholars, parks of sweet-smelling trees and palaces full of gold, ivory and art.

Some cities had buildings five storeys high, with running water and inside toilets – none of which London had.

The British were in awe – and greedy for African gold, copper, ivory, steel ... and even their salt and pepper!

But African empires had been trading with foreigners for thousands of years. They hid their gold mines and sold nothing cheap!

North African Empires Through the Ages

North Africa was where the Egyptian, Nubian and Moroccan Empires flourished. It was also once part of the Greek, Roman and Arabic Empires. In the 1500s most of North Africa was part of the Turkish Ottoman Empire.

S A H A R A   D E S E R T

Ethiopian Empire 1270–1974

The Ethiopian Empire grew out of the Kingdom of Axum, which in the third century was as powerful as the Roman Empire. Axum was the first African nation to make its own coins and, when it became a Christian nation, to put a cross on them. Legend says the Ethiopian emperors' ancestors were King Solomon and Queen Sheba. Ethiopia successfully fought off European colonisers.

Hausa Kingdoms 1st–19th century

These kingdoms were once ruled by powerful queens. They sold blue cloth, salt, gold and leather across the Sahara desert to the Middle East, Europe and Britain. The city of Kano (now in Nigeria) was one of the most powerful in Africa.

The Bornu Empire 1396–1893

This was a warlike empire of soldiers, scholars and cattle ranchers. It was friendly with the Turkish Ottoman Empire that had invaded North Africa.

● Kano

Benin City

Ife

The Empire of Mali 1230–1600s

This empire sent ships to South America. One Emperor, Mansa Musa, was the richest man who ever lived. He gave away so much gold once on his way to Mecca that the price of gold in Egypt crashed.

● Timbuktu

The Kingdom of Morocco 788–present day

Once this kingdom ruled Spain and Portugal for more than 500 years. In this era, Britons and Europeans lived in terror of its pirates who kidnapped more than a million people to sell into slavery.

The Songhai Empire 11th century–1591

This was one of the biggest empires in the world ever. It traded in gold, copper, salt and books! Houses in the capital, Timbuktu (now in Mali), had toilets. In London, people were still emptying potties onto the streets!

The Oyo Empire 500 BCE–1750

Knights in armour defended this Yoruba empire. They had rules they lived by – a warrior code. Queen Oluwo paved the capital city, Ife (now in Nigeria), 800 years before London. It is famous for glass, bronze and terracotta art.

AFRICA

The Kingdom of Nri 1043–1911

No violence was allowed in this Igbo Kingdom. They did not need to conquer. Instead, whole towns and villages chose to join them and refugees were welcome.

- Pate (now in Kenya)
- Malindi (now in Kenya)
- Gede (now in Kenya)
- Zanzibar (now in Tanzania)
- Dar es Salaam (now in Tanzania)
- Kilwa (now in Tanzania)
- Comoros

Swahili City States 8th–16th century

For thousands of years, more than 40 cities here traded goods from all over Africa to Europe, the Middle East, India and China. Gold, salt, timber, ivory and steel were swapped for silk, pottery, spices and jewels. For 2,000 years they made the best steel in the world.

The ancestors of most Black British people today come from these great civilisations!

The Matapa Empire 1430–1760

This mighty Empire stretched across the whole of Southern Africa (now Zimbabwe, Zambia, Mozambique and South Africa). Its gold mines were worth billions and its capital, Greater Zimbabwe, was bigger than London was. Its palaces were gilded in gold and full of pottery from China.

Sofala (now in Mozambique)

The Benin Empire 1100s–1897

The capital city, Benin (now in Nigeria), was protected by walls longer than the Great Wall of China. It was full of gold, ivory and bronze art. Inside the walls, the city was completely safe – the buildings did not even need doors! Its people were honest, peaceful and polite.

The Kingdoms of Kongo 1390–1857

Armies of archers protected these powerful kingdoms, and armies of administrators collected its peoples' taxes. The kingdoms had ambassadors in Europe and Queen Nzinga forced back invading Europeans for years.

THE AMERICAS

The wealth of foreign lands like Africa and India was trickling into Britain and Europe. But the kings and queens wanted more – and wanted it quickly!

In the 1500s, British ships sailed to West Africa and then found their way to India. They began trading there in 1600.

But, while looking for India in 1492, the Italian explorer Christopher Columbus had bumped into the Americas. He thought he had found India and called the Caribbean 'the West Indies'.

North and South America and the Caribbean are called the Americas. Britain and other European nations fought over them for hundreds of years. They killed most of the people there, destroyed their civilisations and made them colonies. Britain eventually conquered North America and made it a colony.

Most people who moved here from Britain (and elsewhere in Europe) were fleeing poverty, famine, religious attacks and invasions. The ancestors of most white Americans were refugees. They treated the Native Americans like they had been treated, and worse.

Spanish ships sailed back from South America loaded with stolen silver and gold. Queen Elizabeth I was so green with envy that she commanded her knights to capture those ships. Those knights became the queen's pirates and were called sea-dogs!

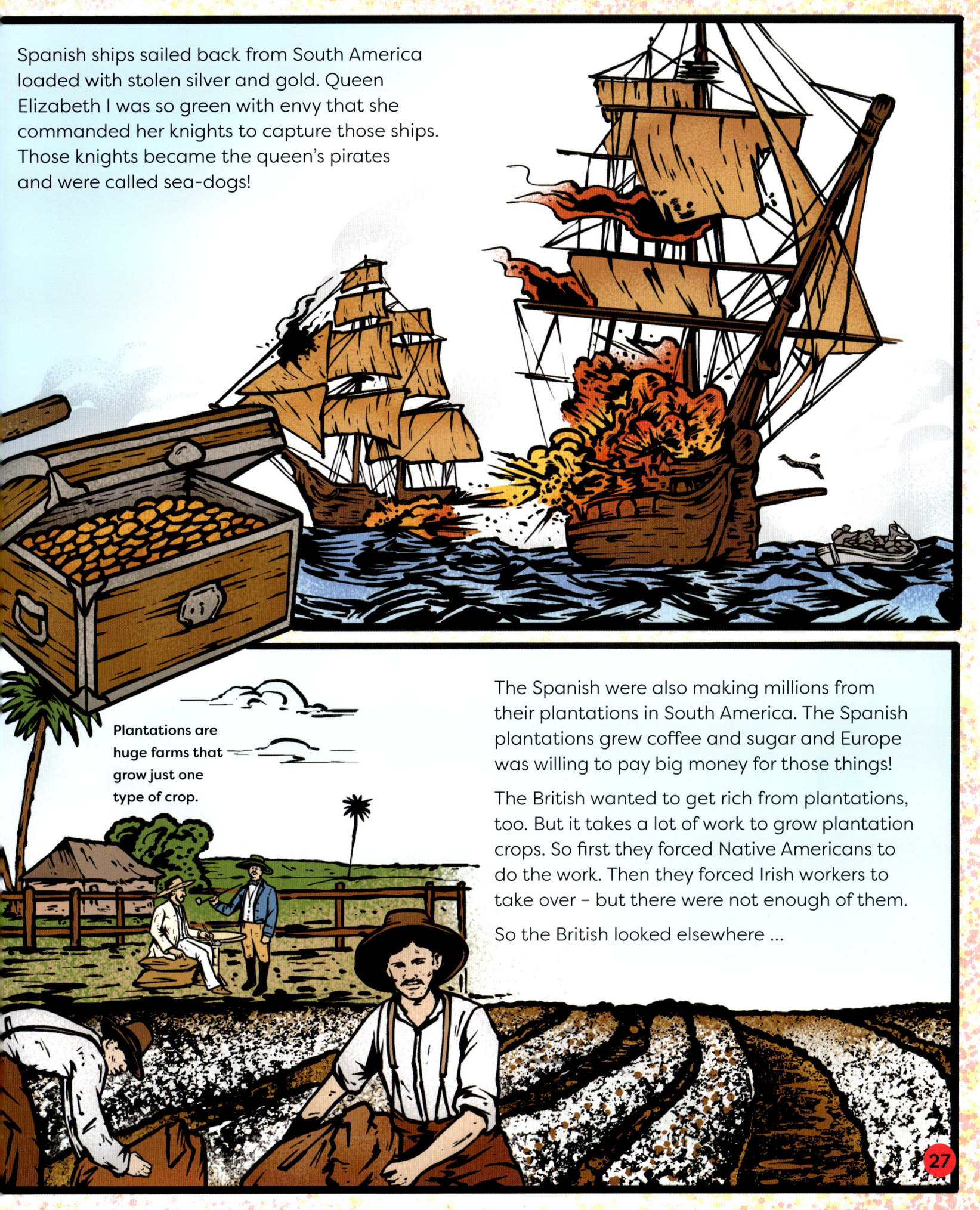

Plantations are huge farms that grow just one type of crop.

The Spanish were also making millions from their plantations in South America. The Spanish plantations grew coffee and sugar and Europe was willing to pay big money for those things!

The British wanted to get rich from plantations, too. But it takes a lot of work to grow plantation crops. So first they forced Native Americans to do the work. Then they forced Irish workers to take over – but there were not enough of them.

So the British looked elsewhere ...

STOLEN PEOPLE

The greed for plantation profits led to the most terrible crime in British history.

In the 1600s, Britain copied other European nations and joined in the worst period of slavery that the world has ever known. In the slave trade, Britain stole and sold more people than any other nation.

Many African people tried to stop this – but the British were unstoppable. They had trading buildings along the African coast that they turned into fortresses with cannons.

At first, the British bought prisoners that African rulers had captured in wars with enemy kingdoms.

Then, the British caused wars to make sure there were lots of prisoners to buy.

They also paid kidnappers to snatch men, women and children – sometimes setting fire to villages and seizing people as they ran.

Millions of people were captured, chained together and marched down to the coast where British ships were waiting.

The stolen people were terrified. Most of them had never seen white people before. To them, the white people looked like devils, or evil spirits. And they acted like them, too!

The British sailors forced the stolen people down into the holds of the ships. They were crammed together with no toilets and no windows. The air was so bad, people died. Millions of men, women and children died on British and other European ships in sickness, sorrow and fear. They were thrown to the sharks.

The survivors were dragged off the ships in the Americas and sold to plantations. There they were forced to work. They could not leave and were not paid. Their friends, family and even their children were sold to other plantations. They never got to go home.

Britain stole 3.1 million people. But only 2.7 million made it off the ships alive. And most stolen people who got to the plantations did not live longer than ten years. They were worked, beaten, starved and tortured to death.

7 Then the ships sailed back to Britain.

6 The ships were now loaded with sugar, coffee, tobacco and cotton crops from the plantations – crops grown by the stolen people.

5 When the ships reached the Americas, the people were sold to plantation owners. The ship owners and slave-trading companies made huge amounts of money.

4 Now the ships headed to the Americas, packed full of stolen people.

THE TRIANGULAR TRADE

Britain did not start the slave trade but it grew to be the biggest slave-trading nation in the world. Selling stolen people made Britain rich. England and Scotland became especially wealthy.

8 In Britain the plantation crops were sold. The plantation owners made huge amounts of money.

1 Ships sailed out of ports like London, Bristol, Liverpool and Glasgow carrying goods made in British factories.

2 They sailed to the West African coast.

3 Here, the British goods were swapped for prisoners of war or to pay kidnappers for stolen men, women and children. The factory owners made huge amounts of money.

BIG BUSINESS

The Royal African Company in Britain bought and sold more African people than any other slave-trading company in Europe. It was owned by King Charles II, his brother the Duke of York and other British royals and aristocrats. It made them super-rich.

The factory owners got rich because some Africans wanted their fancy new goods. Those Africans did not know the fate of the people they sold.

The plantation owners got rich because they did not pay their workers. They also grew addictive crops like sugar, coffee and tobacco, which Europe just wanted more of.

People all over Britain owned stolen people on plantations in the Americas. They were paid for the work of those stolen people!

REBELLION

Stolen African peoples never stopped fighting for their freedom – either on the slave ships or on the plantations.

Some chained people were freed by African warriors before the ships set sail. Other times, the stolen people took over the ships on the journey to America. In 1752, on the British ship Marlborough, the captives took over and won a gun battle against another slave ship that tried to stop them sailing home.

The stolen people took no possessions from their homes to the Americas. But the memories of their cultures and traditions kept them strong.

They trained secretly in traditional African martial arts, disguised as dances, like capoeira.

They told African folktales of tricksters like the spider Anansi, who knew how to fool the powerful.

And they made up songs with African rhythms and chords to give them courage, and pass on secret escape codes.

32

Great leaders like Nanny Grigg in Barbados and Tacky in Jamaica organised rebellions on the plantations. At first they failed – but they never gave up. The stolen people rebelled again, and again, on every island and in every county in the Americas!

Those who escaped hid up in hills or down in swamps where they could not easily be caught. They built their own villages and towns, fought against slavers, and helped others escape, too.

Some stolen people ended up in Britain, even though there were no plantations. Most were forced to work as servants or sailors. Many of them were only children.

Many of those who managed to break free led remarkable lives. They were authors, sportsmen, entrepreneurs, composers and musicians. And they fought to help others like themselves.

If your ancestors survived slavery, be proud! They were some of the strongest, bravest, most resilient people on the planet.

Mary Prince was the first woman to present an anti-slavery petition to parliament. She was also the first Black woman to publish her own life story.

BLACK GEORGIANS

Now came the Georgian era in Britain, when four kings were called George, one after the other!

During the Georgian era, the small ports that slave ships sailed from grew into big cities. And the rich got even richer from the triangular trade. They built country mansions and fancy townhouses for themselves, and some built hospitals and schools for the poor.

Most British people at that time were so poor they were glad to get a job as a servant for the rich. It meant regular money, food and a roof over their heads.

For many rich Georgians, it was fashionable to have a stolen Black child serving them.

Other Black Georgians were in every walk of life. There were even elected MPs, like James Townsend and Richard Beckford.

Some Black Georgians had been in Britain for generations, and were free. Others were the few who managed to escape slavery.

The oldest Black communities in Britain today started in the Georgian Era in Liverpool, England, and Cardiff, Wales.

Thousands and thousands of Black people lived in Georgian Britain. In fact, more than 3 million white people in Britain today have Black Georgian ancestors!

Bill Richmond
I was a celebrity boxer. King George IV invited me to his coronation.

Queen Charlotte
I became queen when I married King George III. The court commented on my Black features and many modern historians believe that I had African ancestry.

Joseph Antonio Emidy

I was one of the top violinists at the Opera House in Lisbon, Portugal. British sailors kidnapped me and brought me to Cornwall.

Olaudah Equiano

I was kidnapped from Nigeria as a child. I fought for my freedom and became the first Black employee of the British government.

Ayuba Suleiman Diallo

I was a scholar before being stolen. I wrote out the Quran from memory. I am the only person on record, out of 3.1 million people stolen by Britain, to go home. My portrait is in the National Portrait Gallery, London.

Charles Ignatius Sancho

I was born on a slave ship. I became a brilliant writer and composer. I was the first Black man on record who voted in Britain at a time when most white people were not allowed to vote.

Captain John Perkins (Jack Punch)

I was the first Black officer in the British Royal Navy. I captured 315 enemy ships. A record!

RACE

By the end of the Georgian era, people all over the world were saying that slavery was wrong. But it was making powerful people so rich that they promoted a new idea they hoped would make slavery seem okay.

Some European philosophers had come up with the idea that Homo sapiens – our human race – was not one race, but several different races. Their idea was that some races were better than others. And what race you belonged to depended mostly on your skin colour.

These philosophers had white skin, so, of course, they chose the white race as the best one. This is now called white supremacy.

They said people with black skin belong to the worst race – so it was okay to force them into slavery.

Those philosophers – and their followers – somehow convinced people that the amount of melanin in a person's skin affects the cleverness of their brain, the goodness of their hearts and their value as a person!

This is now called racism.

Scientists say that race is just an idea – it is not science. 99.9 per cent of every single person's DNA is the same. And Homo sapiens are one race – with both good and bad in every single person.

ABOLITION

Black activists like Ottobah Cugoano, Ignatius Sancho and Mary Prince campaigned to stop slavery. Some white people, such as a man called Granville Sharp, joined them in the fight. They were called abolitionists.

Jonathan Strong, a stolen and abused Black London teenager, begged Granville Sharp for help. Granville helped Jonathan, then studied law and wrote a book that proved slavery was against the law in Britain.

Did Granville know that Lord Mansfield and his wife did not have children? Did he know that they brought up two beloved nieces instead?

One of them was Dido Elizabeth Belle. Her father was Lord Mansfield's nephew and her mother was a stolen woman from Africa – Maria Belle.

So one of Lord Mansfield's beloved nieces was Black!

Granville got lawyers to use his book to argue against slavery in front of the most important judge in the whole country – Lord Chief Justice Mansfield.

After listening to Granville's lawyers in 1772, Lord Mansfield got as close as he could to making slavery illegal in Britain.

But was it Granville who made up Lord Mansfield's mind? Or Dido?

THE INDUSTRIAL REVOLUTION

Hundreds of years after slavery began, stolen people were still being forced to work on British plantations in the Caribbean. And in America a new crop was being grown: cotton.

Growing cotton was backbreaking work, done by the stolen plantation workers.

The raw cotton was then shipped to Britain and bought by factory owners in the north of England.

New technologies like the spinning jenny (a wheel for spinning wool or cotton) made it possible for factories to turn the cotton into cloth much more quickly than before.

Cotton cloth was very popular. It is easy to wash and dry, more comfortable than wool and cheaper than silk. The whole world wanted it!

By this time, America was not ruled by Britain anymore. It had won a war of independence in 1783.

When the steam engine was improved in 1765, factory owners could now send the cloth all over the world on steam trains and steam ships.

Cotton cloth became Britain's biggest export (something a country makes and sells to other countries). It made Britain rich!

The steam engines ran on coal, so new coal mines opened, mostly in South Wales, the Midlands and the North of England.

Poor British farm workers came from the country to work in the mines. Millions moved to work in cotton factories in the cities, too.

This was called the Industrial Revolution.

The workers were hoping for a better life. But they were paid so little that even their children had to work – or starve to death.

Most children were working 12 hours a day by the time they were ten, and some by the time they were six. Many died from breathing in cotton fibres, and from accidents and injuries from the machines – there were no health and safety rules then.

Thanks to cotton, American plantation owners made a fortune. So did British factory and mine owners. And Britain became a superpower – the first industrialised nation in the world.

But who did all the work?

FREEDOM

The triangular trade had gone on for nearly 300 years. All that time people were being stolen, and suffering and dying. But they were also still fighting for their freedom.

- On the island of Haiti, there was rebellion after rebellion. In **1804**, the enslaved people finally drove the plantation owners off the island and everyone in Haiti was free!

- In **1831**, 60,000 plantation workers in Jamaica went on strike and burned plantations down. Their leader, Sam Sharpe, said they would not go back to work until they had both some freedom and wages. But, once again, the army forced them back.

- In **1823**, 10,000 plantation workers in Guyana put down their tools. But the army killed hundreds and forced the rest back to work.

- Armed with farm tools, the enslaved people rebelled. Each time, the owners called in the nearest army to shoot the rebels dead. But the rebellions continued.

- In Britain, many ordinary people put pressure on the government to ban slavery abroad.

  Some people gave up eating sugar grown on plantations. Cotton factory workers went on strike, risking starvation. Women organised meetings, protests, petitions and fundraising even though they were not allowed to vote.

- The Sons of Africa, a Black abolitionist group, and the white MP William Wilberforce argued for parliament to ban slavery.

  But the British parliament dug in its heels. Many politicians owned plantations in the Caribbean. They said Britain would not thrive without the profits of slavery.

This, on top of the work of British abolitionists, meant that in **1807**, the British Parliament were forced to sign a ban on the triangular trade once and for all. Then Britain got to work stopping other nations from kidnapping people from Africa, too!

But people already on the plantations were forced to stay. And so were their children, and their children's children – for 15 generations or more!

The Royal Navy sailed off to chase down slave ships with their cannons blazing! The people on the ships were returned to the African coast.

Stolen people were now free – but with no money, no land and no help. Many Black communities and countries are poor to this day.

In the end, parliament had to give in. At long last, in **1833**, slavery was banned in the British Caribbean – and other countries followed. In **1865**, slavery in America came to an end, too.

Britain (and America) paid huge compensation – not to the stolen people, but to those who had 'owned' them instead.

THE COST OF SLAVERY

1 in 4 people on slave ships were children.

15 generations of people or more were enslaved.

315 years is how long Europe stole people from Africa.

46,000 Britons 'owned' stolen people when slavery ended.

800,000 stolen people were on British Caribbean plantations in 1833.

2,000,000 stolen people died at sea.

4,000,000 stolen people were on American plantations at the time slavery ended.

12,500,000 people, at least, were stolen by Britain and Europe.

THE VICTORIAN ERA

An 18-year-old young woman called Victoria became the queen of the United Kingdom four years after slavery was banned. Queen Victoria ruled from 1837–1901. In those 63 years, Britain changed more than ever before.

Black builders

Black nannies

Black coal miners

Black servants

Superintendent Robert Branford, police officer

Agnes Foster, charity worker for the Salvation Army

At the beginning of the Victorian era, most people in Britain lived on farms and the fastest way to get around was by horse. But that was about to change! It was an era of inventions all over the world, when inventors were making life easier for everybody.

Elijah McCoy, a Black Canadian-American, studied engineering at Edinburgh University in Scotland. He went on to invent a way to oil steam engines that made trains much faster and cheaper. Railways were built from city to city in Britain.

Arthur Wharton, footballer

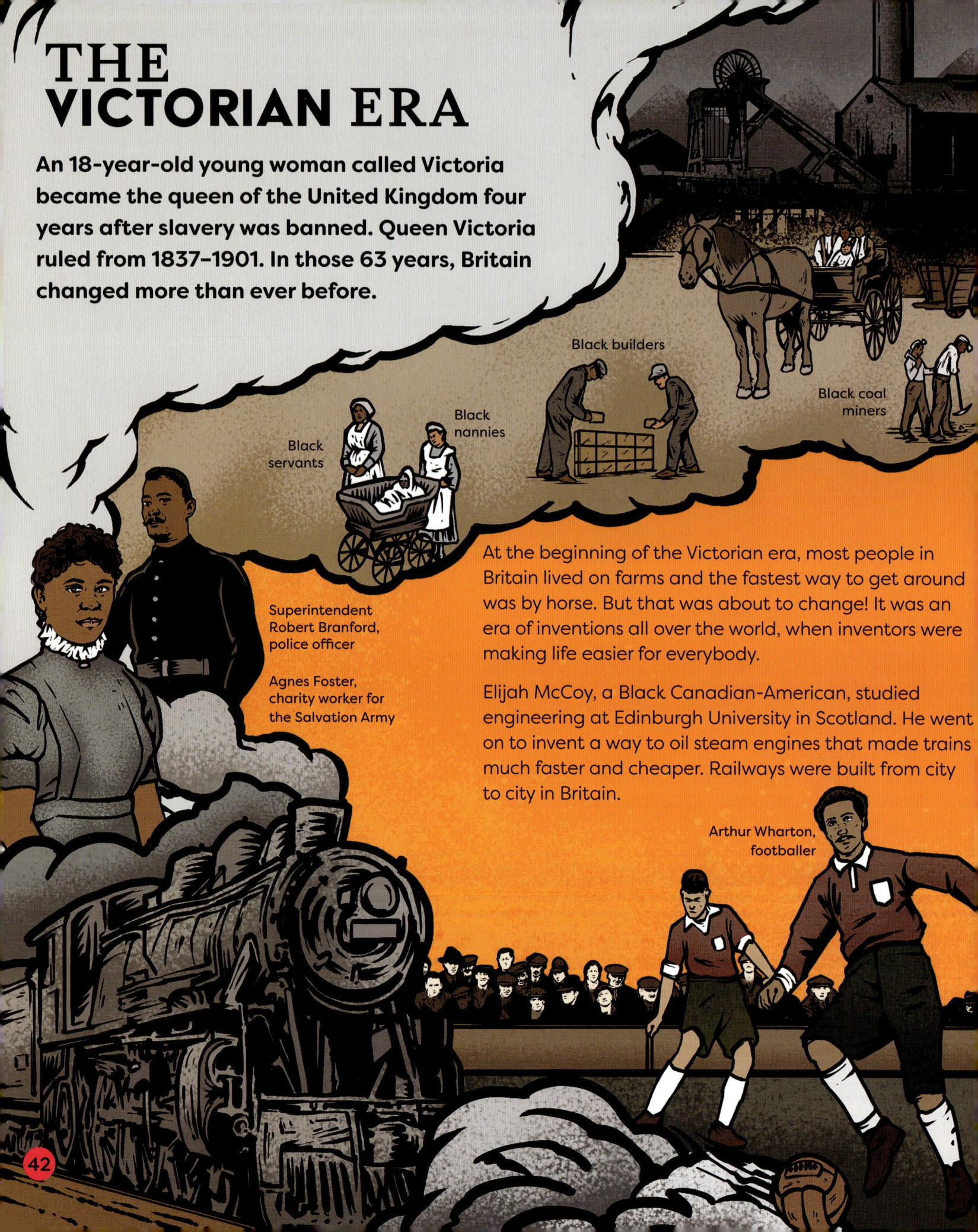

ROYAL CONNECTIONS

Queen Victoria had two famous Black godchildren: Nigerian-born Sarah Forbes Bonetta and the Ethiopian Prince Alemayehu. She sent Alemayehu to boarding school. It must have been incredibly hard to be the only Black child there. He died at just 18, some say of sorrow.

Another Black American, Lewis Latimer, made light bulbs long-lasting enough to be affordable. He also supervised the installation of electricity in London.

There were thousands of Black Britons in the Victorian era, mostly in London, Liverpool, Bristol, Cardiff and Glasgow. Some were celebrities: famous musicians who travelled the world, footballers who broke records, circus owners and war heroes. Some were politicians, like Peter McLagan, who served as Scotland's first Black MP in 1865. Other people did ordinary jobs, like being nannies or builders. In the Victorian era, Black Britons did every kind of job!

Olga "Miss LaLa" Brown, Polish circus performer who toured Britain

Pablo Fanque, circus owner

Arnold "Kid" Sheppard, boxer

Sergeant William Dobson, drummer in the 72nd Highlanders

George Bridgetower, musician and composer

Samuel Coleridge-Taylor, composer

THE BRITISH EMPIRE

During the Victorian era, Britain's empire grew to be the biggest in the world. The money from slavery had made Britain a rich superpower. Now slavery was abolished, the country had to look elsewhere for riches. And it found them in the countries it had conquered and the countries it was about to conquer – its colonies.

Many of the Crown Jewels in the Tower of London were stolen from former British colonies.

Before the British Empire, most people in Britain could not afford sugar, tea, coffee or chocolate, let alone gold jewellery or diamond engagement rings. But the British Empire changed all that!

England loved colonising other countries. In the Middle Ages, England conquered Wales. Before the Georgian era, England forced Scotland to merge with it. And before the Victorian era, Ireland was officially conquered. Together, these countries became the United Kingdom.

America was a British colony before it became independent. And parts of the Caribbean and Canada were British colonies, too. Britain even colonised Australia! That is why English is spoken in those countries.

In every country that Britain colonised the same things happened: the people whose country it was were either killed, driven away or forced to work and pay taxes to the British. The British took their land, their freedom and their riches.

When India became a colony, goods like tea, rice and jewels, as well as taxes, flowed back to Britain, while in India millions of people starved to death.

The same thing happened in other colonies – including Ireland and Scotland. England left most people there without enough to survive. Millions fled to America as refugees.

Britain took the tea in China and the oil in the Middle East. And in the late 1800s Britain joined Europe and invaded Africa.

Britain and Europe had become rich and powerful from slavery, industry, warfare and the stolen wealth of colonies. With this power, they were able to conquer 10,000 African kingdoms and divide Africa into just 40 countries.

When the British invaded Benin City (in Nigeria) they blew up the great city walls, burned peaceful houses and tore the palace apart to get the treasures. Nigeria is still trying to get them back.

Britain took everything that Africa had to offer – gold, diamonds, iron, copper, coltan, cocoa, timber and more.

By 1913, the British Empire covered nearly a quarter of the world!

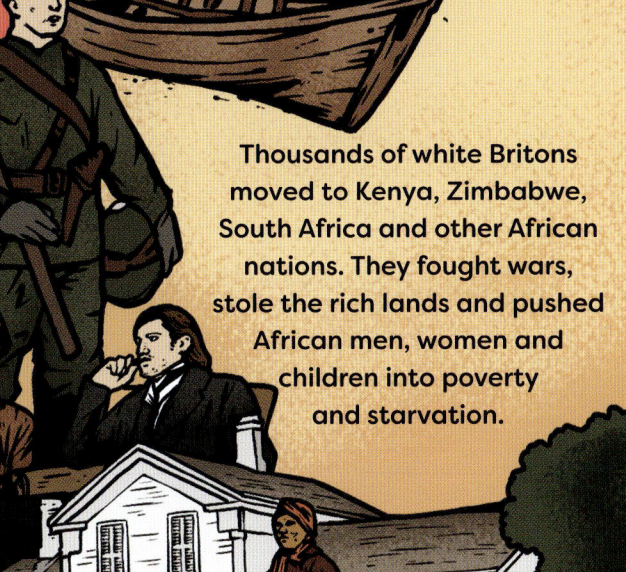

Thousands of white Britons moved to Kenya, Zimbabwe, South Africa and other African nations. They fought wars, stole the rich lands and pushed African men, women and children into poverty and starvation.

During the Great Famine in Ireland, about 1 million people died while food was shipped from Ireland to England.

Without copper from Central Africa there would not be electricity in every home in Britain. And without the mineral coltan from the Congo, there would be no mobile phones or tablets today. Many children are forced to work as miners.

STOLEN RICHES

Not only did the British Empire cover almost a quarter of the world, but for 400 years, it also stole wealth from that quarter of the globe and shipped it back to Britain.

People from Africa and South-East Asia came to Britain on the ships, too. They were mostly sailors and students who settled in Cardiff, Edinburgh, Glasgow, Liverpool, Bristol and London.

The Empire took new words from these continents as well, to add to hodgepodge English.

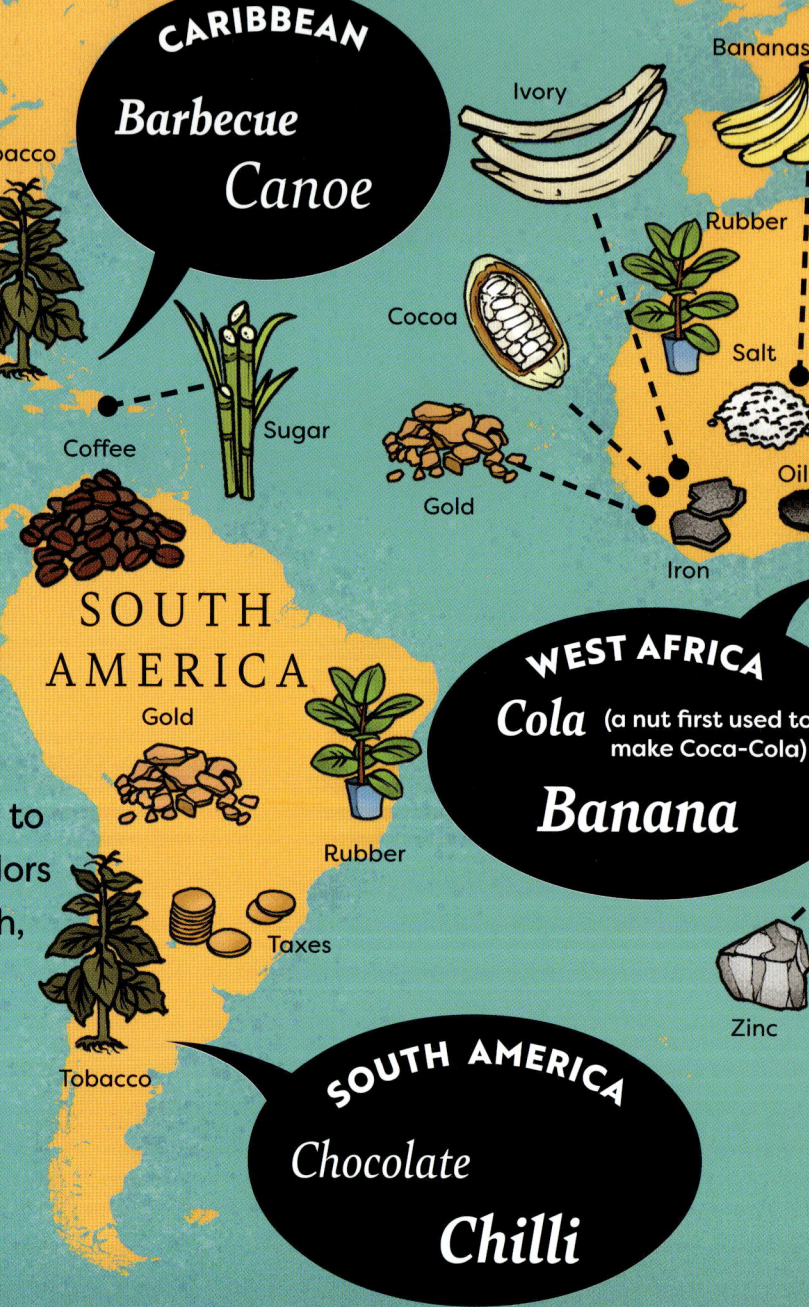

EMPIRE GOODS

Look at the map to see the goods that Britain stole. These goods are still used to make lots of things we have in Britain today. As an example, cocoa butter is used to make chocolate, soap, shampoo, lipstick and even some medicine.

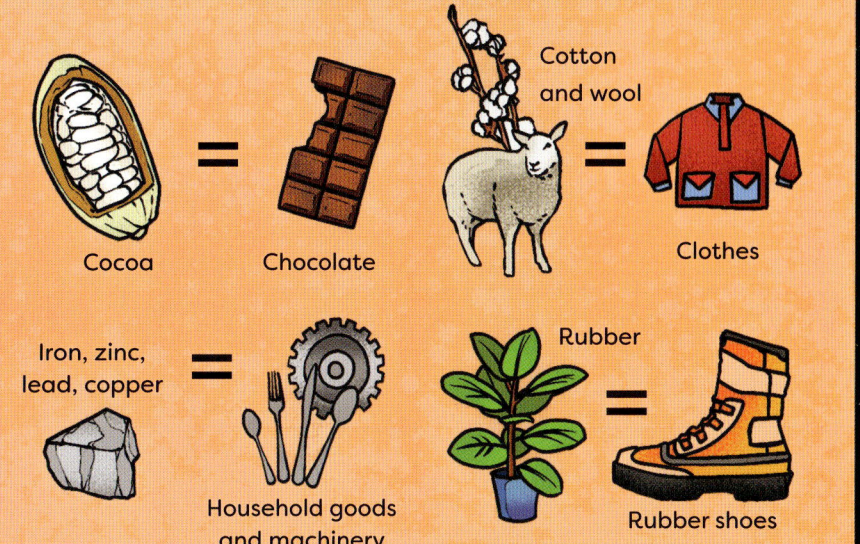

Cocoa = Chocolate

Cotton and wool = Clothes

Iron, zinc, lead, copper = Household goods and machinery

Rubber = Rubber shoes

Tea

Jewels

ASIA

Textiles

Spices

Taxes

CHINA
Ketchup
Tea

Tea

Cotton

Oil

Coffee

Taxes

Textiles

AFRICA

Tea

EAST AFRICA
Safari

Gold

Copper

Salt

Lead

Diamonds

INDIA
Bangle *Bungalow*
Avatar *Jungle* *Curry*
Pyjamas
Dungarees
Shampoo

Spices

Jewels

Coal

AUSTRALIA

Iron

Gold

NEW ZEALAND
Kiwi

AUSTRALIA
Boomerang

Wool

WORLD WARS

In 1914, Europe exploded into a war over colonies. Britain took sides with France, Russia and others against Germany, Austria-Hungary and others. They all made their colonies fight each other, too. And so it became a world war – World War One.

World War One lasted for four long years. In Europe the soldiers dug trenches to shelter from guns, bombs and poison gas.

The Royal Air Force fought sky battles using a new invention: aeroplanes. The Royal Navy fought with another new invention: submarines.

There were thousands of Black men in the British troops. Some were from families born in Britain and were sons of miners, sailors, lawyers and doctors.

Armies of African soldiers were forced to fight for Britain on the African continent.

Thousands of others volunteered to fight from the colonies of the Caribbean. Workers also came from faraway China. But most of the soldiers from the Empire came from India. Three million soldiers from the Empire fought on Britain's side.

At the end of World War One, more than 20 million people had died. Many were only teenagers. The side that Britain was on had won. And there was peace again ... but only for 21 years.

Germany was broken by the war. But a new leader called Adolf Hitler came to power who said he could make Germany great again.

When his soldiers marched on other countries, Britain and France got together to stop him.

And so, in 1939, another world war began.

About 150,000 Black American soldiers came to help Britain. A Black American, Dr Charles Drew, invented a way to store and ship blood. It saved the lives of thousands of sick and injured Britons – and still does.

Soldiers from African countries were forced to fight again – but many volunteered, too. And so did people from the Caribbean and India.

They wanted to stop Hitler, who was killing Jewish and other minority peoples, and win the right to run their own countries, too.

Bombs were dropped on British cities and thousands of people were killed. Children, Black and white, were sent to live in the countryside.

British women of all colours worked together in factories, farms, hospitals and war offices.

After six years, the side that Britain was on won again. But 60 million people had died worldwide.

BLACK HEROES

Black soldiers, Black doctors, Black farmers, Black spies, Black inventors ... so many Black British, Black Caribbean and Black African people helped Britain to keep its freedom by winning the wars.

THE HEROES OF WORLD WAR ONE

Harold Brown, England

I was a London teenager who fought on the battlefields even when I was wounded. I won a Military Medal for bravery.

Roy and Norman Manley, Jamaica

We were brothers who fought in the trenches. Roy was killed, aged 21. Norman won a medal and became prime minister of Jamaica.

Sergeant Robbie Clarke, Jamaica

I was the first Black pilot to fly for Britain. I was shot while on a spy mission but somehow managed to fly back to safety.

Lieutenant Walter Tull, England

I was a professional footballer who once played for Tottenham Hotspur. I was the first known Black officer in the British Army.

THE HEROES OF WORLD WAR TWO

Amelia King, England

I would not take no for an answer so I got to work for the Land Girls, helping farmers grow food for Britain.

Lieutenant Johnny Smythe, Sierra Leone

I volunteered after I read Hitler's book. When my plane was shot down I managed to parachute out. I became Attorney General of my country.

Tommy Douglas, Wales

I was from Tiger Bay in Cardiff. I went to war at 14 and died when a submarine sunk the ship I was on.

Princess Ademola, Nigeria

I was invited to London for the coronation of King George VI. I stayed on as a nurse during the Blitz (when British cities were heavily bombed).

Ita Ekpenyon, Nigeria

I was in charge of air raid shelters in Marylebone, London. I helped hundreds of people escape from bombs.

Sid Graham, England

My ship was sunk by a submarine. Me and my mates were stuck on a lifeboat for ten days with sharks circling.

Dr Cecil Clarke, Barbados

I kept my GP surgery open every day, even when it was bombed. My formula for safe dosages of medicine for children is still used today.

Princess Tsehai, Ethiopia

I was a nurse and the daughter of the Emperor of Ethiopia. I looked after sick and injured children in London during the Blitz.

Una Marson, Jamaica

I worked for the BBC on a popular radio show to keep British spirits up.

THE WINDRUSH GENERATION

It took all of Britain's money to win World War Two. Afterwards, the cities were left in rubble and most people were extremely poor. More than 2 million British people migrated to other countries.

The National Health Service (NHS) was set up in 1948 to help people who could not afford to pay for doctors or medicine. The government took over organising the buses and trains to make sure people could get to work.

But there were not enough doctors and nurses for the NHS, or conductors for buses and trains, or engineers and labourers to rebuild the cities. Britain needed help!

EMPIRE

LO

Sam Beaver King, Mayor of Southwark, London, first used the phrase 'Windrush Generation'.

So the government asked people from the colonies to come. The NHS, London Transport and British Rail put job adverts in Caribbean newspapers. Lots of people came. They were British citizens. Their countries had been left poor after slavery and colonisation and they wanted good jobs to make better lives for their families.

Most came to Britain by ship. The first and most famous ship arrived in 1948. It was called the *Empire Windrush*. Caribbean people who moved to Britain after the war are called the 'Windrush generation'.

Soon Caribbean people were joined by many more Black people from Africa. They came mostly from the countries of Nigeria and Ghana at first, and then from Kenya, Uganda, Zimbabwe and Somalia. Lots of South Asian people came too, from India, Pakistan, Bangladesh and from some African countries.

Everyone who moved to Britain after the war brought their skills, their cleverness and their hard work to help Britain get back on its feet.

The NHS would not have survived without the thousands of amazing doctors and nurses from the Caribbean, Africa and India.

THE COLOUR BAR

The courageous people who came to Britain from the colonies were shocked by the poverty, the rain and, worst of all, the racism. The government had asked them to come, but British people did not seem to want them.

When Black people tried to rent rooms, buy houses or get good jobs, most white people said no!

When this happened, Black people worked hard to find other solutions. They set up their own Saturday schools and savings schemes.

Saying no to someone because of the colour of their skin was called 'the colour bar'. It existed long before people arrived on the *Windrush*.

In **1965**, the government made the colour bar illegal in public places.

In **1964**, when a pub would not serve Black people, Paul refused to leave until they did. He was arrested for causing trouble but the court said he was innocent. The Prime Minister wrote to Paul promising to stop the colour bar.

In **1968**, the colour bar became illegal in jobs and housing, too. But many shops – like high-end ones on Oxford and Regent street in London – still would not employ Black people to serve customers.

Activist Jocelyn Barrow was not going to stand for that! She called them out, and, with help from the Jewish head of Marks & Spencer, forced them to offer jobs to Black people.

The police made life difficult too, stopping and searching Black people and their businesses.

In **1970**, the Mangrove Nine organised a protest against police stopping and searching people and were arrested. The judge found them innocent. He said the police were racist!

The Colour Bar before *Windrush*

Way back in the **1800s**, Black nurse Mary Seacole was not allowed to work in British army hospitals. So she went out to help on the battlefields on her own and set up a hostel for soldiers.

● In the early **1900s**, Black doctor Harold Moody could not get a doctor's job, even though he received top grades at medical school. So he set up his own surgery in Peckham, London. He later started an organisation to fight the colour bar with war hero, Dr Cecil Clarke, a Black gay GP.

● By the **1960s**, the colour bar was still a problem. A bus company in Bristol, England refused to employ Black or Asian drivers. So, in **1963**, a youth worker called Paul Stephenson started the Bristol Bus Boycott, where he asked the people of Bristol not to travel on the bus. So many people stopped using the buses that after four months the company had to change its mind.

During the **1900s**, some white people rioted and attacked Black people. From **1962**, the government brought in laws to make it harder for Black people to move to Britain.

● During the **1980s**, some young Black people protested. They were fed up with having no good jobs or good housing and were angry with the police for bullying them.

● In **1981**, there was a big protest called the National Black People's Day of Action. Thousands of people came.

In a historic election in **1987**, the British public voted in three Black MPs – Bernie Grant, Paul Boateng and Diane Abbott.

People like Harold Moody, Jocelyn Barrow and Paul Stephenson fought to end racism – and together they changed Britain for the better.

Antigua and Barbuda

Gabon

The Bahamas

Barbados

Bangladesh

Belize

Botswana

Brunei

Cameroon

Canada

Cyprus

INDEPENDENCE

While people in Britain were fighting the colour bar, people in the colonies were fighting British rule. They wanted to rule their own countries. They wanted independence.

The colonies fought with both words and guns, and eventually most of them won their freedom. The British Empire came to an end. But even today there are countries ruled by England where some people want independence.

For those countries who got independence, things were still not easy. After hundreds of years of slavery and colonisation – with no compensation – they were poor.

Dominica

The Gambia

Guyana

Grenada

India

Malaysia

Lesotho

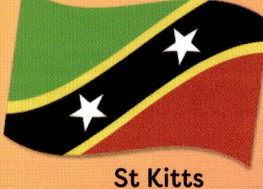
St Kitts and Nevis

Kenya

Eswatini

Jamaica

When countries got their independence, many of them joined the Commonwealth – a group of countries who believe in peace, democracy, freedom and development. These are the flags of the Commonwealth. Most of these countries were once part of the British Empire.

United Kingdom

Trinidad and Tobago

Malta

Malawi

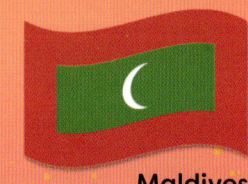
Maldives

Mauritius

Mozambique

Namibia

Nauru

Togo

New Zealand

Pakistan

Papua New Guinea

Nigeria

Rwanda

St Lucia

Samoa

Seychelles

Even now the wealth of those countries – oil fields, mines and plantations – is still often owned by British and other foreign companies. Most of them pay their workers so little that even some children have to work, while the profits go abroad. Companies that call themselves 'fairtrade' pay their workers fairly.

There are also other problems. Colonised countries were made by joining ancient kingdoms together. Now people in the same country speak different languages to each other, and have different religions, cultures and traditions. This can often make it hard for them to get along and sometimes leads to civil wars.

Sierra Leone

Solomon Islands

Singapore

When there is war and poverty, people run away from their countries. Those who come to Britain do so in hope of a better life. They know Britain is rich – it took their countries' riches. Britain also once boasted to its colonies that it was the land of hope and glory.

Sri Lanka

South Africa

Tonga

Kiribati

Ghana

Tuvalu

St Vincent and The Grenadines

Many African freedom fighters were once students in Britain, like Kwame Nkrumah who became Ghana's first president.

Uganda

Vanuatu

Tanzania

Australia

Zambia

BLACK BRITISH CULTURE

The history of the British people is the history of migrants.

Each group of people who moved to these grey-green, rainy islands – the Stonehenge builders, the Celts, the Romans, the Anglo-Saxons and more – brought with them a new culture that changed Britain.

Modern Black people from Africa and the Caribbean have brought their cultures, too!

London's **NOTTING HILL CARNIVAL** is one of the biggest Caribbean carnivals in the world! It began in the 1960s to celebrate the joy, culture and music of the Caribbean.

Most modern British music is **BLACK MUSIC**. Soul, R&B, rock-'n'-roll, hip hop and garage began as Black American music. Reggae began in the Caribbean and Afrobeats in West Africa. They led to original Black British music like jungle, drum and bass and grime. Music by white musicians like The Beatles and Ed Sheeran use Black music styles. So many Black British musicians, like Winifred Atwell, Shirley Bassey and Sade, were superstars. And megastar Stormzy raps and sings, mixing grime, gospel, R&B, soul and Afro-styles to take the world by storm!

Most **BLACK CHURCHES** are full of gospel music. In fact, it was Black gospel singers in America who started rock-'n'-roll music!

gal dem
man
BRUV
Bredrin
fam

Black people have changed the English **LANGUAGE** by bringing new meanings to old words. Black Americans reinvented words like 'cool' and 'chill'. Jamaicans did the same with words like 'fam', 'bruv', 'man' and 'galdem'. Black British English is spoken all over Britain.

Black British people from African countries brought their **HAIRSTYLES** to Britain, making box braids and extensions popular. They also brought their bright fabrics and make-up, and helped liven up British fashion!

RASTAFARIANISM is a modern Black religion from Jamaica, famous for its peaceful lifestyle and dreadlock (locs) hairstyle. Locs became a common hairstyle in Britain. A famous British Rastafarian was the poet Benjamin Zephaniah. British band Soul II Soul helped make locs popular in America!

Traditional African art inspired famous white artists like Picasso and led to what is called **MODERN ART**. The Blk Art movement was started in the 1980s to make sure modern Black artists got noticed, too. Now Black British artists, such as Chris Ofili and Lubaina Himid, win top prizes.

In 2021, Black British people were four per cent of the population in England and Wales – but Black culture is so popular that it has changed British culture and language FOREVER!

Akeim Mundell

By day, Akeim is an assistant headteacher. By night, he's a hero who finds jobs for people so they don't have to turn to crime for cash.

Alex Wheatle

This children's author started reading in prison. Now he writes books about kids in care (like he was) and who live on council estates.

Alice Dearing

Alice is an Olympic marathon swimmer. She started the Black Swimming Association and wears swim caps especially made for Afro hair.

Anne Mensah

Anne has chosen what programmes get made for British TV in her top jobs at Netflix, Sky and the BBC.

Dr Chris Jackson

This professor of geology has climbed up mountains and into volcanoes – and presented science programmes on TV.

Dr Christopher B. Lynch

Christopher worked as a hospital porter before becoming a doctor. He invented an operation that has saved the lives of millions worldwide.

David Lammy

David was a lawyer who became an MP when he was only 27. He's been fighting for people's rights in parliament ever since.

Prof David Olusoga

This historian makes new discoveries about British history and talks about them on his popular TV shows.

Edward Enninful

Edward is a fashion stylist and head of British Vogue magazine. He puts Black faces on the covers of top fashion magazines.

Dr Elaine Arnold

Elaine is a social worker and university lecturer. She says migrant children suffer loss that can make them angry or silent.

BLACK PEOPLE MA

Dame Prof Elizabeth Anionwu

This professor of nursing taught the NHS how to treat sickle cell anemia – saving thousands of lives.

Marvyn Harrison and Elliott Rae

These men help fathers in Britain be the best dads they can be through books and podcasts.

Evelyn Forde

Evelyn left school without qualifications but went back when she was grown up. Now she is an award-winning headteacher.

Gary Younge

Gary is an award-winning reporter, author and professor. He reports on issues many others ignore.

Ismail Ahmed

Ismail was a refugee before starting a money transfer company to help people send cash abroad. It is now worth billions.

Jacky Wright

Jacky comes from a big Caribbean family in London. She used to work for the tax office. Now she works in America as one of the heads of Microsoft.

Jamal Edwards

Jamal started the music platform SBTV, which helped make musicians like Ed Sheeran and Skepta famous.

Jawahir Roble

Jawahir is a football coach and men's games referee. She says refereeing taught her to stand up for herself.

Kadiatu Kanneh-Mason

This Welsh-Sierra Leonian raised seven children who are all classical musicians. Her son Sheku played the cello at Harry and Meghan's royal wedding.

Leroy Logan

Leroy joined the police to try to stop racism. Actor John Boyega plays him in a film by Steve McQueen.

Lewis Hamilton
Lewis is one of the greatest Formula One drivers ever. He has won the British Grand Prix eight times.

Dr Maggie Aderin-Pocock
Maggie struggled at school with dyslexia. Now she is a space scientist. She designs machines that go up into space.

Malorie Blackman
Author Malorie's work was rejected 82 times, but she did not give up. She has now written more than 70 books, and TV shows, too.

Marcus Rashford
This Manchester United player fought the government to provide free school meals for kids going hungry – and he won!

Marsha de Cordova
Being blind does not stop Marsha. She studied law before becoming an MP. She fights in parliament for the rights of all her constituents as well as people with disabilities.

Martin Griffiths
This trauma surgeon from Lewisham saves the lives of njured people. He also works to stop gang violence.

Na'ima B. Robert
Na'ima writes children's books and works to inspire women. She wears the niqab so she is judged for her words and actions, not her looks.

Naomie Harris
Naomie is an award-winning actress who plays lead roles in both James Bond and *Pirates of the Caribbean* films.

Nicola Adams
Nicola was the first woman to win an Olympic gold for boxing and the only woman to win all four world titles.

Prof Nira Chamberlain
Nira won the title 'World's Most Interesting Mathematician'. Thanks to him, the Royal Navy were able to build their biggest ship ever.

KE BRITAIN GREAT

Pat McGrath
This leading make-up artist has influenced fashion make-up worldwide. She has her own brand.

Patricia Gallan
This high-ranking, medal-winning Scottish policewoman says poverty causes crime and believes Britain needs to become fair and equal.

Patricia Scotland
Patricia is a top lawyer and politician who worked to make it a crime to be violent in the home. She is Secretary-General of the Commonwealth.

Paulette Rowe
Paulette has worked in top jobs for banks and payment companies. She was named as one of the most influential women in finance in the world.

Rosalie Jones
Rosalie was a small, sick child. But she became a firefighter, saving British lives for more than 30 years.

Dame Sharon White
Sharon has run huge companies like John Lewis and Ofcom. She also helped run the Treasury of the government.

Sheldon Mills
This Welsh lawyer makes sure small businesses and shoppers get fair deals. He defends the rights of LGBTQIA+ people, too.

Solomon Golding
Solomon grew up in London, Jamaica and Ghana. He was the first Black British born dancer in the Royal Ballet company.

Stephen Akpabio-Klementowski
Stephen had no qualifications – but he took exams in prison. Now he's a university lecturer and out of prison.

Wilfred Emmanuel-Jones
It took 40 years for Wilfred to fulfil his dream of being a farmer. Now his brand 'The Black Farmer' is in most supermarkets.

BLACK **LIVES** MATTER

Although race does not scientifically exist – and every human's DNA is 99.9 per cent the same – racism still exists today.

Statistics tell us that Black people are still often turned down for jobs and university places. They show that Black people are stopped more often by the police and sent to prison when white people, who have committed the same crime, are not.

This is called institutional racism.

Racist laws still exist. And some of the Windrush generation who the government asked to come to help Britain have been sent back – to countries where they no longer have jobs, homes or family.

In 1993, a British teenager called Stephen Lawrence was murdered – just because he was Black. When the police did not send the murderers to prison, his mother Doreen Lawrence did not give up! She fought to prove that the police had not done their job properly because they were racist. And she made sure two of the murderers did go to prison in 2012.

There have been deaths like Stephen's all over the world. And in 2020 when a Black American man, George Floyd, was murdered by a white policeman, suddenly people had had enough!

Black Lives Matter protests happened in countries all around the world. Millions of people of all skin colours marched to say that Black lives matter to them.

In 2020, four young people of colour organised a BLM protest in London's Hyde Park. Thousands of people of all skin colours came. More marches also happened all over Britain.

Black sportspeople started going down on one knee, known as 'taking the knee', to show their sorrow over racism. Now people of all skin colours take the knee to show their sorrow and respect.

One day, racism will be over. People continue to fight. Famous people fight racism, such as Stormzy, who pledged £10 million to the cause. Ordinary people can change the world, too – Jonathan Strong, Granville Sharp, Mary Prince and Doreen Lawrence all did.

What will you do?

ABOUT THE AUTHOR

Atinuke wrote her first story when she was five years old. It's always been her favourite thing to do. She lived in Nigeria as a child, in England as a teenager, and is now based in Wales. Atinuke used to tell old African folktales to audiences all over the world. Now she spends her time writing stories of her own – stories that have been turned into more than 20 books for children!

ABOUT THE ILLUSTRATOR

Kingsley was inspired by his architect dad and loved drawing as a child – he especially loved making comics. He was born in Italy before moving to Britain. When he was little, Kingsley dreamed of being able to draw all day. Now Kingsley is an artist, illustrator and designer who loves to study old oil paintings in his spare time!

GLOSSARY

abolition Ending or stopping something completely.

activist Someone who takes action to make the world a better place.

ancestors A person's parents, grandparents and great-grandparents going back in time.

BCE Before Current Era, or CE. Before the year 1 according to the calendar used in Britain.

CE Current Era. From the year 1 onwards according to the calendar used in Britain.

creed A religious belief.

colonisation One country taking over another country.

colony A country that is controlled by another country.

empire Group of countries or regions ruled by just one country or ruler.

enslavement The act of taking control of another person and their entire life.

ethnic group A group of people with shared ancestors and culture.

migrant Someone who moves from one place in the world to another.

pagan A person with religious beliefs that are not part of main world religions like Judaism, Christianity or Islam.

profit Money left over after a business' costs are paid.

racism The belief that some 'races' are worse than others, and treating those people badly.

refugee A person seeking safety in another country.

trade Swapping or selling things.

LEARN MORE ...

Black and British, An illustrated history, 2021
Black and British, A short, essential history, 2020
both by David Olusoga
The Black History Book, DK, 2021
Black History Matters, Robin Walker, 2021
Black in Time, Alison Hammond, 2022
The Black Curriculum books
www.theblackcurriculum.com

A NOTE ON THE TEXT ...

In this book, we spell the word 'Black' with a capital 'B' when it refers to people or cultures who have some or all African ancestry. (Some people with African and other heritages refer to themselves as 'brown'.)

We spell the word 'black' with a lower case 'b' when we refer to Cheddar Man and the first Britons because they were from an ethnic group that no longer exists. Scientists call them the 'Western European Hunter-Gatherers'.

AUTHOR THANKS ...

With thanks to my amazing mother RJA for her enormous help. And to Kingsley for pouring so much life into the powerful illustrations. And to my patient consultants – Kehinde Andrews on history, Jasmine Richards on sensitivity and Tom Booth on science. And to those scholars whose incredible discoveries are within these pages – David Olusoga, Robin Walker, Miranda Kaufmann, Stephen Bourne, authors of The Oxford Companion to Black British History (2007) and the scientists at the Natural History Museum, London.